THE HALLOWEEN BOOK OF FACTS & FUN

Wendie Old

Illustrated by
Paige Billin-Frye

Albert Whitman & Company
Morton Grove, Illinois

Also by Wendie Old and Paige Billin-Frye:
The Groundhog Day Book of Facts and Fun

For my sisters, Sandy and Marion, and my brother, Don.
Didn't we have fun trick-or-treating together?—W.O.

For the Slusarczyks.—P.B.-F.

Library of Congress Cataloging-in-Publication Data

Old, Wendie C.
The Halloween book of facts and fun / by Wendie Old ; illustrated by Paige Billin-Frye.
p. cm.
ISBN 10: 0-8075-3133-2 (hardcover)   ISBN 13: 978-0-8075-3133-4 (hardcover)
1. Halloween—Juvenile literature. I. Billin-Frye, Paige, ill. II. Title.
GT4965.O53 2007 394.2646—dc22 2007001342

The design is by Carol Gildar.

For more information about Albert Whitman & Company,
please visit our web site at www.albertwhitman.com.

Thanks for riddles to:
Dian Curtis Regan (pp. 13, 15); Rick Walton (pp. 30, 39 [Lake Eerie riddle]); Jane Yolen (pp. 5, 39 [Vampire State Building riddle]).

Table of Contents

Chapter One

Halloween Night

There's a knock on the door. Should we open it or not?

Peek through the window—oh, no! Monsters and princesses, soldiers and angels, robots and aliens are at the door, shouting "Trick or Treat!"

It's October 31, Halloween. Masked children are attacking the neighborhood, demanding candy and treats.

Neighborhood families are prepared for this attack. They have supplies of wrapped candy and toys ready to hand out. Sometimes the whole family enjoys this holiday so much that they decorate their yard with Halloween symbols. Witches. Ghosts. Spiders and spider webs. Black cats and bats. Skeletons and gravestones. Dracula and Frankenstein. Pumpkins carved with beautiful designs or scary faces.

Weird music whispers behind the bushes. Sometimes puffs of fog float around the children's feet. Perhaps even a coffin lies near the door with a vampire rising out of it.

But the children aren't scared—much. They scream, but keep on walking to the next house.

Most of the kids walk in groups. Younger ones are with their parents.

What is an October hot dog called?

A Hallowienie.

They move from house to house, chanting "Trick or Treat!" If the house has a front porch light on, they know it's okay to ask for treats. If the light is off, don't bother.

Everyone carries a plastic pumpkin or a bag to hold the loot. Some older children carry pillowcases, hoping to get a lot of treats.

Knock, knock.

"Trick or Treat!"

Even very young children quickly learn that this magic chant will make candy appear.

How did this strange celebration come to be?

Chapter Two

The Origins of Halloween

Halloween began long ago as part of the Celtic new year festival. Tribes of people we now call Celts (KEHLTS) lived in Ireland, Great Britain, and northern France about twenty-five hundred years ago. Their festival marked the end of summer and the coming of the dark, cold winter. Since the Celts worshiped the gods and spirits of nature, like the sun god, this was also a time to thank their gods for the harvest.

The Celts called the festival Samhain (SAH-win), which means "the end of summer." Samhain was celebrated during the three days of the full moon close to the end of the month we call October. To symbolize the end of the summer half of the year, all fires in the house were put out. Later, the Celtic priests, called Druids (DROO-ids), created a new fire for the new year. The villagers carried hot embers from this central fire to relight the fires in their homes.

The Celts believed that during the period of fireless darkness between the ending of summer and the beginning of winter, ghosts of the dead, as well as other-world beings such as spirits and faeries, crossed over from the spirit world into our world.

The Celts also believed that during this time between seasons, the past, present, and future mixed. Predictions about the future could be made. Druid priests would ask the spirits about things that affected the whole group: Will the crops be plentiful next year? Individuals asked questions about their own futures: Whom will I marry? Fortune-telling games played on Halloween today have their beginnings in the belief that the future could be foretold on Samhain.

About two thousand years ago, the Romans conquered the Celtic people in France and the part of Britain we now call England and Wales. They did not conquer Ireland, but spread their culture there. The Romans brought along their own gods and goddesses. They also planted apple trees and introduced their goddess of fruit trees, Pomona. Her feast day was November 1, close to the festival of Samhain. Over the years, Roman traditions, such as using apples

8

to predict the future, mixed with Celtic traditions.

In one Roman game, girls cut a symbol or their initial into apples, then floated them in tubs of water. The boy who could bite a girl's apple and pull it from the water might end up marrying her. At some Halloween parties today, children still play a similar game—bobbing for apples.

Over the following centuries, a new religion called Christianity grew in France, Britain, and Ireland. In the 800s, the Christian church established November 1 as the holiday of All Saints' Day, or All Hallows' Day—a day to celebrate the lives of the saints of the Christian religion. ("Hallowed" means "holy.") October 31, the evening before All Saints' Day, became known as All Hallows' Eve—or Halloween.

All Saints' Day was meant to eventually replace Samhain, but the old Samhain practices continued for many years. The church later added a second holy day on November 2 and called it All Souls' Day. On this day families pray for the souls of their loved ones who have died.

Even when most of the Celts had converted to Christianity, they kept the belief that all manner of spirits roamed the land on the night of October 31. Today, these "spirits" can still be seen in the spooky costumes and decorations we love on Halloween.

Chapter Three

Why Do We Wear Costumes and Trick-or-Treat?

During Samhain, people wore costumes for a variety of reasons. Some dressed in brown and green—the colors of branches and leaves—to look like nature spirits. They wore masks to disguise their faces. They hoped that if they wore masks and danced away from the village, any angry spirits who had shown up at this time would follow them and leave the village alone.

Other villagers dressed in gray as if they were the ghosts of people returned from the dead. Some dressed in animal skins, complete with the animal's head or a paper head representing it. These costumed people knocked on doors asking for food. The people in the house pretended not to know who was under the costume. Special treats were set aside for the visitors.

Becoming Christians didn't stop the Celts from observing these and other old traditions. Groups of boys raced from door to door, rattling the latches. They chanted a song asking the housewife to give them bread, butter, and milk, which they would then cart away to a party in

What instrument does a skeleton play?

A trom-bone.

the woods. Older boys and men in costume demanded beer and snacks.

An underlying threat was there. If the household did not give out food, drunken visitors might come back and cause mischief. What kinds of mischief? Perhaps they might let the cows out of the barn, set fire to the roof-thatch, or even damage the crops in the field. In the morning, the mischievous spirits of the night could be blamed for the destruction.

Groups of girls gathered inside for parties, playing games they thought might foretell the future.

Often Christian customs were celebrated along with Celtic traditions. Sometimes beggars went from house to house on All Souls' Day (November 2). They would ask for soul cakes—special cakes baked this day to honor the souls of family members who had died. Their song indicates that other food would have been welcome, too, perhaps including beer or wine.

> *Soul! Soul! For a soul cake!*
> *O pray you good mistress, a soul cake.*
> *An apple, a pear, a plum or cherry,*
> *Or any good thing to make us all merry.*

Centuries later, in the 1840s and 1850s, more than a million immigrants came to the United States from Ireland. Their own country could not support them because of the potato famine. The main Irish food crop at that time was the potato—and because of disease, the potatoes were rotting in the fields before they could be harvested. The Irish came to find jobs and a new life in the United States. These immigrants brought Halloween traditions based on the ancient festival of Samhain.

As time passed, however, Halloween became just a time to have fun.

When children go from house to house today with costumes and masks, chanting "Trick or Treat!" many historians believe they are carrying on the old Celtic traditions of wearing disguises and begging for food on All Hallows' Eve and All Souls' Day.

Chapter Four

The Tale of Jack-o'-Lantern

Of all the symbols of Halloween, the pumpkin is most popular. Almost every house in the United States displays one, carved into a jack-o'-lantern with its flickering grin. But because there once were no pumpkins in Ireland, people there used hollowed-out turnips or large beets. This is the story of the very first jack-o'-lantern.

How do you mend a broken jack-o'-lantern?

With a pumpkin patch.

A long time ago, a man named Jack lived in Ireland. Hard work was not for him. And Jack was mean, stingy and mean. He'd kick a dog if it didn't move fast enough out of his way. He ate by helping himself to pies left out to cool and eggs in someone else's henhouse. Sometimes, he'd be so mean that even his soul wanted to get away from him.

One Halloween evening, Jack had fallen asleep. His soul had just backed out of his body and was hovering over it, thinking about drifting away and not coming back, when who should notice this but the devil himself.

POOF!

13

The devil appeared beside the sleeping Jack and grabbed for his soul. The soul, not really wanting to leave this earth, slipped back into Jack's body and Jack woke up.

"Hey!" Jack yelled. "I'm not ready to go yet!"

The devil just stood there, tapping his foot. "Really?" he said.

"Really," Jack argued. "I need one drink before I go with you."

"All right," said the devil. "Are ye sure ye have enough money for a drink?"

Jack looked into his purse. All he had left was a sixpence. He needed two sixpence to get a drink. What could he do?

"I know," he told the devil. "You can turn yourself into another sixpence. Then I can pay for the drink." Jack knew it would be easy for the devil to change himself back after the money was paid to the bartender.

The devil liked the idea of cheating the bartender. POOF, he turned into a sixpence lying on the road. Jack smiled. He picked up the sixpence and dropped it into his purse. He clicked that purse shut, and the devil was caught and couldn't get out. Why? Because when the purse's clasp was turned shut, it became the shape of a cross. The devil cannot touch this Christian symbol.

When the devil discovered he could not get out, he began to yell and curse.

"If you want to get out," said Jack, "we have to make a deal. Leave me alone for a year."

14

What's round, orange, and flies?

Superpumpkin.

Of course, the devil agreed. A year is a long time for a human, but just the blink of an eye to the devil.

Jack opened the purse and the devil whizzed out. There was a clap of thunder as the crack to the other world closed behind him.

Jack was sure he'd reform during that year and then the devil couldn't touch him. But he didn't. He slipped back into being mean.

Right before the next Halloween, Jack had just stolen a turnip from a neighbor's garden. He was digging out its center to eat when he dropped dead.

He couldn't enter heaven because he had been so mean. When he knocked on the gates of hell, the devil took one look at him and locked the gates.

"Go on back where ye came from!" he yelled. The devil wanted nothing more to do with Jack because he had come out on the losing side when they'd met before.

"It's dark out here!" Jack yelled back. "How can I see my way?"

"That's your problem. No, wait. Here ye go." The devil picked up a burning coal from hell to light Jack's way and tossed it to him.

"How am I gonna carry that?" muttered Jack. He pulled the stolen turnip from his pocket. Quickly, he scooped up the coal and tossed it

into the hollow place in the turnip. He whipped out his eating knife and poked some holes into the turnip to let the light shine out. It was a long, dark journey back to Earth, and this light would be better than nothing.

When Jack arrived back on Earth, he was a soul without a body. All he could do was wander from place to place, with just this small lantern to light his way.

Jack of the Lantern is a ghost now, one of many drifting through the Halloween night. In the marshes and fields, you can sometimes see his spark flickering hither and yon through the mists. That spark never dies. It just fades, then shows up somewhere else.

In Ireland, many people used to put turnip lights on porches and in windows on Halloween night. Some said it was to give Jack a replacement in case his turnip light burned out. Better to lose a turnip light than to have Jack's ghost haunt you for the rest of the year.

Others said they placed the glowing vegetables to show Jack (and other ghosts wandering loose this night) that they were not welcome.

If you see Jack's light, don't follow it. It might lead you into dangerous, swampy places.

How to Carve a Pumpkin

1. Find the perfect pumpkin.

2. Ask an adult to cut the lid. With a paring knife, he or she should cut a circle about two to three inches from the stem. Cutting at an angle, with the knife pointing toward the center of the pumpkin, will create a shelf for the pumpkin lid to rest on. Lift the lid off. Trim the strings from the bottom of the lid.

3. Take a large spoon and scoop out all the strings and seeds until the cavity is clean and almost smooth. You can clean and dry the seeds to save them for planting next spring or for roasting and eating the nutmeat inside them.

4. Give the adult the pattern you would like on your pumpkin—a smiley or scary face or perhaps a cat, spider, or other creature—and ask him or her to carve it for you.

5. Place a small tea light in the bottom of the pumpkin.

6. Place your pumpkin on your porch or windowsill and have an adult help you light the tea light candle.

7. Place the lid back on your pumpkin and enjoy the flickering glow.

18

Chapter Five

Witches

Think of the word "witch" and you see in your mind an ugly old woman dressed in black. She wears a tall pointed hat and rides a broom. She enjoys causing trouble for people through the evil magic she brews in her black cauldron, and she uses animals, usually a black cat but sometimes a toad or mouse, to help her cast her spells.

These images of witches come from stories like "Hansel and Gretel" and *The Wizard of Oz* or from William Shakespeare's play *Macbeth*, where three witches cook up their wicked spell, chanting,

> *Double, double toil and trouble;*
> *Fire burn, and caldron bubble.*

Actually, the word witch comes from the Old English word *wicce* (for women) and *wicca* (for men), meaning "wise one." Many centuries ago, the wicca or wicce was often the healer in the village, someone who knew what plants could cool a fever or heal a nasty cut. These healers followed a Celtic religion. Through its ceremonies and rituals, they tried to persuade the gods and spirits of nature to protect them.

Most people then believed in magic, both for good and evil. Life was hard and very uncertain. Many people died young; even doctors didn't know how to treat most sicknesses; and when crops failed, people starved. People believed that someone's bad magic caused

sickness and accidents, sudden death and famines. The wicce or wicca seemed able to both turn away misfortune or cause it. They also gave advice and even predicted future events. They were important and respected in their communities.

Who shares a witch's apartment?

Her broommates.

Gradually, practicing magic became associated mostly with women.

From 400 c. e. through 1400 c. e., as the Christian religion spread across Europe, Great Britain, and Ireland, it overpowered the older religions. To convert villagers to Christianity, church leaders declared that the old nature religion that the wicce and wicca (now called witches) followed was really devil worship.

Over the centuries, witches became looked upon as evil creatures rather than healers. Many people even came to believe that witches joined with the devil at meetings called Sabbats, which they reached by flying through the air on pitchforks or broomsticks. Halloween was a special night for witches, as one of the Sabbats was supposed to take place on October 31.

From about 1480 to 1780, there were "witch hunts" in many places in Europe. Anyone could be accused of witchcraft by his or her neighbor. Many accused others out of envy or spite, and those accused were often poor and friendless old women. These innocent women were tortured until they confessed to practicing witchcraft. Then they were executed. During this time, thousands of "witches" were killed.

The settlers who came from England to America in the 1600s brought the belief in witchcraft with them. The largest witch hunt in America took place in Salem, Massachusetts, in 1692. Twenty people were executed, and many sent to prison.

The belief in witchcraft gradually died away in America and Europe, though it still exists today in some parts of the world. There are families today in the United States who follow the old nature religions and call themselves Wicca. But they do not try to harm other people.

On Halloween, it's fun to dress up as a witch and pretend to have magical powers, at least for one night in the year.

How do witches tell time?

With their witchwatches.

Chapter Six

The Truth about Frankenstein and Dracula

Many people enjoy horror stories. During the summer of 1816, the famous English poet Lord Byron and a group of his writer friends were on vacation in Switzerland. Among them were the poet Percy Bysshe Shelley and Mary Wollstonecraft Godwin, who later married Shelley.

To entertain themselves at night, the friends read stories aloud—scary stories. Lord Byron challenged the group to see who could write the scariest one. During the next year, Mary, who was only nineteen, wrote one of the most chilling monster stories of all time—*Frankenstein; or, The Modern Prometheus*. Her book was published in 1818.

People are often surprised to learn that the monster's name was not Frankenstein. In Mary's story, Victor Franken-stein, a student, tried to create new life out of parts of dead people. He created a living, thinking being, but abandoned it because it was horrible-looking.

Everyone who saw this monster either ran from it or threatened it with weapons. It came to hate itself and its creator. The description of the monster's agony and the people it killed has kept countless readers awake at night. It's no wonder that the book has stayed popular all these years.

The first of dozens of movies about Frankenstein's monster came out in 1931. Over the years, the monster has become a favorite character for kids on Halloween. But the green Frankenstein's monster mask that kids like to wear at Halloween is not the face of the monster described in Shelley's book. The mask is based on way the monster has been shown in movies.

Vampires are another popular Halloween monster. Belief in vampires exists in many cultures around the world. Traditionally, vampires were people who were evil in life. After death, they rose from the grave and attacked the living by sucking out their blood.

Probably the most famous book about vampires is *Dracula* by Bram Stoker, published in 1897. This is the tale of Count Dracula, a vampire from a country called Transylvania. Dracula comes to England and sucks the blood from a woman named Lucy. She dies and becomes a vampire, too. Lucy's friends slay the vampire she has become. Then they pursue Dracula back to Transylvania to destroy him.

Ever since Stoker's book, people have used vampires as villains and even heroes. Over one hundred sixty movies and some TV shows have been based on *Dracula*, from silent films in the early 1900s to "Buffy, the Vampire Slayer."

Which monster flew a kite in a lightning storm?

Benjamin Franklinstein

Even children's shows have characters based on Dracula. Count von Count on "Sesame Street" carries on the tradition that vampires love to count tiny things (even grains of sawdust). Count Chocula advertises a cereal!

The legend of Dracula is probably based on the true story of Vlad Dracula III. Vlad ruled a small state in Europe called Wallachia in the fifteenth century. He was supposed to have enjoyed watching his enemies being killed in the most painful way possible. By the time he died in 1476, he had killed somewhere between twenty thousand and one hundred thousand people in his country.

The current holder of the title "Count Dracula" is Ottomar Rudolphe Vlad Dracul Prince Kretzulesco. Ottomar also loves blood. He is a Red Cross volunteer in Germany and runs blood drives!

Chapter Seven

El Día de los Muertos

In the Christian calendar, All Hallows' Eve, or Halloween, is followed by All Saints' Day (November 1) and All Souls' Day (November 2). People in many countries visit cemeteries on these two days and honor their dead. It is a serious time of reflection on the permanence of death.

But people in Mexico and other Latin American countries also joyfully celebrate the lives of their dead loved ones. They call their celebration "El Día de los Muertos" (El DEE-ah day lohs MWEHR-tohs)—the Day of the Dead. Immigrants from these countries, especially Mexico, have brought the festival to the United States.

This is not a time of fearing ghosts and spirits. It is a happy time, a fiesta to remember and celebrate the lives of family and friends who have died.

Graves are cared for. Weeds are pulled and flowers and candles placed there. The flowers can be real or bright paper or silk. Things the dead person loved are put around the grave for him or her to enjoy—a bottle of soda pop or tequila, a violin, a wedding photograph, a piñata, a favorite toy or food. At night the cemeteries glitter with candles and resound with the noise of partying.

Children love the candies and bread (*pan de muerto*) of this fiesta. The sugar candies are in the shapes of skulls and bones. Sweet breads come in funny shapes. Decorations often include tiny hand-painted skeletons doing whatever people loved to do when alive. There could be:

    a mariachi band of skeletons
    skeletons dressed for a wedding
    a skeleton racecar driver

El Día de los Muertos was originally a Native American festival in parts of Latin America honoring the dead. When the Spanish invaded what is now Mexico in 1521, their priests looked to see what parts of the native religion were similar to European Catholic beliefs. El Día de los Muertos seemed similar to All Souls' Day, when Catholics prayed for their dead loved ones. The Spanish conquerors folded this three-thousand-year-old festival into their Christian celebration.

Another tradition of El Día de los Muertos is the decorated altar for the dead in people's homes. The family places things on the altar that represent the four elements of nature—earth, wind, water, and fire.

Since the souls of the dead can be fed by smelling food, earth is represented by offerings of food.

Wind is represented by something that will move in a breeze, such as festive tissue-paper flowers. Often the altars will be surrounded by either real golden-yellow marigolds or paper ones.

The souls of the family dead are thirsty from their long trip home, so a glass of water is placed on the altar.

And fire comes in the form of a candle. There can be many candles on the altar, one for each dead relative. And many people light an extra candle, just in case they forgot to include someone.

All these things on the altar surround pictures of the dead relatives. The family plays their loved ones' favorite music and eats their favorite foods to honor them.

The festival begins on October 31 and continues until November 2. November 1 is a day to remember dead children, and November 2 is the day to remember dead adults.

Chapter Eight

Halloween Today

The Celtic festival of Halloween became popular in America around 1850, after many Irish came to live in the United States. Along with food and decorations, they also introduced costumes and mischief-making. As in Ireland, much of the mischief was meant to be simple pranks, but some became annoying or downright dangerous.

In 1920, the people in Anoka, Minnesota, decided they were tired of finding their windows soaped, cows let loose in the streets, and even their outhouses (outside bathrooms) tipped over or destroyed.

To give children and teenagers something better to do, civic leaders decided to stage a parade. The whole town joined to make costumes and decorations.

How can you tell a baby ghost?

He's wearing boo-ties.

Businessmen donated hundreds of bags of popcorn, peanuts, and candy to give out after the parade.

Nowadays, Anoka calls itself "the Halloween capital of the world." There are two parades with bands from four schools plus fireworks and house- and window-decorating contests.

Other cities began having Halloween

parades and decorating contests, too. The largest parade today is the Greenwich Village Halloween Parade in New York City. Over two million people attend the parade, and over four million watch it on TV.

Most cities in the United States have outlawed pre-Halloween activities such as "Mischief Night," during which teens tangled toilet paper in trees, threw eggs at houses, and sometimes burned barns. Today, towns and cities decide which days and even what time of day children and teens can go trick-or-treating.

Once radio became popular in the late 1920s and early 1930s, radio shows often featured some sort of special Halloween event. On October 30, 1938, an actor and director named Orson Welles took H. G. Wells's book *The War of the Worlds*, a story about Martians invading Earth, and dramatized it on his show as if it were really happening. The script was written by Howard Koch.

Orson Welles didn't intend to panic much of the eastern United States. He had dramatized books in his broadcasts before. He began the show with his usual introduction of the book he was going to dramatize. Then an orchestra started to play.

It was Welles's unusual method of presenting the story that panicked people. Many tuned in late. They missed the title of the book and were enjoying the music when suddenly a "newscaster" began breaking into the music with more and more announcements about Martians landing on Earth—in Grover's Mill, New Jersey—and proceeding to march toward New York City. (H. G. Wells's story took place in England.)

Terrified people called their local police. Others called the radio station. Few believed it when told what they heard was only a radio drama.

Cars clogged the narrow highways as people tried to escape the invasion. Some grabbed guns to defend Grover's Mill. People called their relatives around the country, and soon there were rumors of multiple Martian landings. Of course, many people did not hear the show and, the next day, could not believe that so many others had been fooled by a pre-Halloween prank.

Copies of this famous broadcast are still available. Get one from your library or check it out on the Internet and listen to it next Halloween night. See how believable it seems to you.

Today we dress up as monsters or princesses or movie characters on Halloween night. We enjoy hayrides, visiting haunted houses, watching Halloween parades, eating candy apples and candy corn, and pretending to be scared of spiders, ghosts, and graveyards. It's a fun time for children and the young at heart.

Chapter Nine

Have a Halloween Party!

Decorations

- Paper or plastic jack-o'-lanterns on the walls and sitting on tables. An adult could carve a fancy design on a real pumpkin.
- Fake spiders and spider webs are usually available around Halloween (or you could make your own paper spiders and spider webs from string).
- Pictures of monsters, skeletons, and ghosts—funny or scary.
- Other Halloween symbols, such as skeletons, black cats, etc.
- "Haunted woods": glow-in-the dark sticks are available in stores at Halloween. An hour or two before you expect your guests, break the sticks to make them glow. Insert them into white balloons and blow the balloons up.

    Tie the glowing balloons to tree branches or bushes in your yard. To make the balloons look like ghosts, tape tissue streamers on them or place pillowcases over them.

Crafts to Make

- Decorate paper lunch bags with crayons, Halloween stamps, or stickers.
- Make orange construction paper pumpkins with black construction paper eyes, nose, and mouth.
- Decorate spookies (small pumpkins) or pumpkin gourds with thick magic markers.
- Make ghosts. Take a lollipop and cover it with a tissue. Tie a ribbon below the head of the lollipop. With a black marker, place two dots for eyes.
- Have your guests take their crafts home in their decorated bags.

Games

1 Pin the Nose on the Pumpkin.

Supplies: A large paper pumpkin with eyes and mouth; various-shaped paper noses; sticky tape.

Put the pumpkin on the wall.

Take two or three inches of tape and create a circle with the sticky side out. Place on the back of a paper nose.

Blindfold a child, turn him or her around, then aim the child at the pumpkin.

When the child bumps into the paper pumpkin, he or she must try to stick the nose where it's supposed to go.

The one who comes closest to the right spot gets a prize.

2 Witches' Cauldron

Supplies: Black plastic cauldron (or cover a stew pot with black paper); slips of paper, white and colored; large mixing spoon.

Write your guests' names on pieces of white paper and place in the cauldron.

Have your guests give you ideas of silly actions. Write them down on colored paper. Have some extra actions already prepared and read several of them to spark your guests' suggestions. (Examples: hop on one foot three times, or touch your nose with your tongue.)

Place all the action suggestions into the cauldron.

With the large mixing spoon, stir the papers in the bottom of the cauldron.

Now pull one child's name and one action. The child must do the action. Keep going until every child has done one.

3 Fortune-telling

Supplies: Forty or fifty dried, raw, or roasted pumpkin seeds in their shells; a dark-sided box; another container (bag or bowl).

Prepare about twenty very funny questions that can be answered by "Yes" or "No."

Mark an X on both sides of HALF of the shells. The shells with the X will be "No" answers. The blank ones will mean "Yes."

Put the questions in one container and the seeds in a dark-sided box so no one can see what seed they are choosing.

Have a child choose a question from the question pile and read it aloud. Then have the child choose a seed to see what the answer will be.

Sample questions: *1) Will I turn green soon?
2) Did the dog eat my sock?* You could even have the group make up the questions themselves first. Lots of crazy ideas can come out of a group-think.

4 Hot Pumpkin

Supplies: A Halloween "thing" to pass around—a small pumpkin, plastic skull, or mummy's hand; a tape or CD and something to play it on.

Your guests should sit in a circle on the floor. As the music plays, children pass the Halloween "thing" around the circle, acting as if it is hot and must be passed quickly.

Interrupt the music at odd intervals. The person holding the "thing" is out.

Continue until only one person is left.

Refreshments

Candy Skulls

Add a bit of El Día de los Muertos to your Halloween party by letting your guests make candy skulls to eat or take home.

1/3 C. softened butter	1/2 tsp. vanilla
1/2 tsp. salt	1/3 C. clear corn syrup
1-lb. box of confectioners' sugar	squeeze tubes of colored icing

Blend the first five ingredients with a mixer (add sugar slowly).

Roll tablespoons of the candy mixture into one-inch balls.

Shape balls into skulls and press two spots for eye holes.

Decorate with squeeze tubes of red/green/yellow/orange/black icing (found in any grocery store).

(The traditional candy skull recipe is sugar mixed with egg whites. Handfuls of this mixture are pressed into large skull-shaped molds and left to dry, then decorated with frosting.)

Spider Cupcakes

Supplies: Iced chocolate cupcakes; pretzel sticks; squeeze tubes of black icing.

Break four thin pretzel sticks in half.

Let your guests push the eight pretzel pieces (four to a side) into the icing of each cupcake.

Using some of the leftover black icing bought for the skulls, make eyes.

Gloopy Drink

Supplies: Packets of green Kool-Aid; liter bottles of clear soda; small marshmallows; squeeze tubes of black icing; a large bowl.

Mix one packet of Kool-Aid for each bottle of soda.

With the icing, put dots on both sides of small marshmallows.

Float the marshmallows in a bowl. They will look like eyes.

Halloween Safety Tips

🎃 Make your costume large enough so you can wear warm clothing under it.

🎃 Keep the hem six to ten inches from the ground so you don't trip.

🎃 Make your costume light-colored or put on reflective strips.

🎃 Carry a flashlight after dark. Don't carry candles or other flame.

🎃 Don't eat treats until you're back home. In the light, you can check each one to see if it is safe to eat.

🎃 Only knock on doors of homes that have their front lights on.

🎃 Don't enter any homes.

🎃 Walk on sidewalks. Do not cross yards.

🎃 If there's no sidewalk, walk on the left, facing traffic, so drivers can see you and you can see them.

🎃 Tell your family where you're going. Always go in a group with an older teen or an adult.

🎃 Carry a cell phone or money to make a phone call in emergencies.

🎃 Be sure to come home at the time agreed upon. Parents tend to worry!

More Halloween Riddles

What do mummies dance to?

Wrap music.

Where do bloodsuckers live in
New York City?

The Vampire State Building.

What are witches best at in school?

Spelling.

Where do ghosts swim?

Lake Eerie.

Which room do zombies stay out of?

The living room.

Why did Dracula go to the doctor?

Because he was coffin.

Why did the monster gain weight?

He was always goblin.

Bibliography

Adult Books:

Bannatyne, Lesley Pratt. *A Halloween How-to.* Gretna, La.: Pelican Publishing Co., 2001.

Better Homes and Gardens. *Big Book of Halloween,* ed. Carol Dahlstrom. Des Moines, Iowa: Better Homes and Gardens Books, 2003.

Clark, Bridie, and Ashley Dodd. *The Halloween Handbook.* New York: Workman Publishing, 2004.

Cohen, Hennig, and Tristam Coffin, eds. *Folklore of American Holidays.* Detroit, Mich.: Gale Research, 1997. Pp. 427-42.

Friedhoffer, Robert. *How to Haunt a House for Halloween.* New York: Franklin Watts, 1988.

Griffin, Robert, and Ann Shurgin, eds. *The Folklore of World Holidays.* Detroit, Mich.: Gale Research, 1998. Pp. 603-47.

Limburg, Peter. *Weird! The Complete Book of Halloween Words.* New York: Bradbury Press, 1989.

Morrow, Ed. *The Halloween Handbook.* New York: Citadel Press, 2001.

Panati, Charles. *Extraordinary Origins of Everyday Things.* New York: Harper Paperbacks (reissue), 1987.

Ravenwolf, Silver. *Halloween.* St. Paul, Minn.: Llewellyn Publications, 1999.

Rogers, Nicholas. *Halloween: From Pagan Ritual to Party Night.* Oxford, Eng.: Oxford University Press, 2002.

Children's books:

Barth, Edna. *Witches, Pumpkins, and Grinning Ghosts: The Story of the Halloween Symbols.* New York: Clarion Books, 1972.

Gibbons, Gail. *Halloween Is . . .* New York: Holiday House, 2002.

Greene, Carol. *The Story of Halloween.* New York: HarperCollins, 2004.

Hill, Douglas. *Witches & Magic-Makers.* New York: Alfred A. Knopf, 1997.

Hoyt-Goldsmith, Diane. *The Day of the Dead: A Mexican-American Celebration.* New York: Holiday House, 1993.

Merriam, Eve. *Spooky ABC.* New York: Simon and Schuster Books for Young Readers, 1987, 2002.

Internet:

http://cfmb.icaap.org/content/28.3/BV28-3art2.pdf. From the Canadian Folk Music Bulletin web page (viewed April 2007).

http://galenet.galegroup.com. Biography Resource Center, a Thompson Gale Database, powered by InfoTrac (viewed April 2007).

http://www.azcentral.com/ent/dead/history. Miller, Carlos. "Indigenous People Wouldn't Let 'Day of the Dead' Die" (viewed April 2007).

http://www.historychannel.com/minisites/halloween. History Channel—"The History of Halloween" (viewed April 2007).

http://www.spiritualitea.com/articles/briefhistory.shtml. Bonewits, Isaac. "A Very Brief History of Witchcraft I.O." An excellent article, but very scholarly (viewed April 2007).

http://www.washingtonpost.com/wp-srv/national/horizon/oct98/hallo101498.htm. Erickson, Ken C., and Patricia Sutherland. "What's Behind Halloween—Where Our Weird Rituals Originated." Washingtonpost.com, October 14, 1998 (viewed April 2007).

Interviews:

Michael Lawrence's observations of the Day of the Dead celebrations in southern California (August 2006).